ESSENTIAL LIFE SKILLS SERIES

WHAT YOU NEED TO KNOW ABOUT

BASIC WRITING SKILLS, LETTERS & CONSUMER COMPLAINTS

Carolyn Morton Starkey   Norgina Wright Penn

NATIONAL TEXTBOOK COMPANY • *Lincolnwood, Illinois U.S.A.*

Preface

This book gives you what you need to know about basic writing skills and about writing letters, personal memos and consumer complaints to help you cope better with everyday situations. Mastering these reading skills will make you more assertive and self-confident.

You will learn about some familiar yet very important material. The topics in this book include:

topic sentences	capitalization
paragraphs	personal letters
verb tenses	business letters
sentence structure	personal memos
punctuation	consumer complaints

Throughout the book you will find examples of real letters and memos, the type you see and use every day.

Each section in this book includes definitions of words that may be new or difficult. Checkup sections help you review what you have learned. Many opportunities to practice are included throughout. Because of its completely flexible format, the book can be used either for self-study or in a group setting with an instructor. The perforated pages of the answer key make it easy to remove. Thus the book meets the needs of both individuals and groups.

When you have learned the skills in this book, you will want to study other skills that will make you a more knowing person in our modern world. The other books in the Essential Life Skills Series will show you how.

Essential Life Skills Series

What You Need to Know about Reading Labels, Directions & Newspapers 5314-6

What You Need to Know about Reading Ads, Reference Materials & Legal Documents 5315-4

What You Need to Know about Getting a Job and Filling Out Forms 5316-2

What You Need to Know about Reading Signs, Directories, Schedules, Maps, Charts & Utility Bills 5317-0

What You Need to Know about Basic Writing Skills, Letters, and Consumer Complaints 5318-9

Contents

Basic writing

You will need effective written and spoken English skills throughout your life. By now you have probably mastered oral skills. There are a number of reasons why people *understand* you when you speak. You are able to use gestures and facial expressions. You can use your voice to stress words and phrases. Anyone can tell when you are angry or annoyed. Your tone of voice helps to carry the message. Your voice has pitch patterns, too. You raise your voice at the end of a question. You use a lower pitch when you make a statement. People give you feedback, too. The people listening to you respond in some way to what you say. If a person doesn't understand you, the person may frown or raise an eyebrow. A person may even ask, "What did you say?" or "What do you mean?" In speaking you can always *rephrase* what you have said. If you have to, you can start over. A person's response to what you say can let you know if you've said enough or too much.

Written communication is different. No one can hear your voice rise when you ask a question. No one can hear it fall when you make a statement. A person cannot sense any pauses between thoughts. If you use the wrong word, the reader can't stop and tell you he or she is confused. And if you spell the contraction of "there is" as "theirs," the reader may simply conclude that you're not very smart. So it is very important that you learn to *write* clearly.

You will be asked to express yourself in writing many times. In school there are always written assignments. A teacher might ask you to do a research paper, write a report, or take an essay exam. There may be times when you will have to write on the job, too. Social workers write case reports. Secretaries write minutes of meetings. And supervisors often have to write training materials and evaluations. You will need basic writing skills in managing your personal life, too. Both business and personal letters require writing skills. Résumés and job applications require you to write, too. Basic writing skills are a necessary part of adult life. These skills must be mastered if you are to express yourself effectively.

Basic writing word review

WORDS TO KNOW

clause   a group of words which contain a subject and a verb

coherent   describes a clear and logical relationship between sentences

edit   make changes

essay   a piece of writing consisting of several paragraphs on the same topic, with a clear beginning, middle, and end

fragment   an incomplete thought punctuated as a sentence

helping verb   verbs that help the main verb express action or make a statement such as *has* played, *is* coming; sometimes called *auxiliary verbs*

linking   joining; word used to describe the verb *to be*

objects   the word (or word group) which receives the action expressed by the verb in a sentence

paragraph   a part of a composition; a short composition (usually indented) dealing with one idea and containing a topic sentence, support sentences, and a concluding sentence

person   the form of a pronoun which tells whether someone is speaking (first person), is spoken to (second person), or is spoken about (third person)

proofread   review writing for errors

run-on   two sentences running together without an end punctuation mark between them; two sentences separated by a comma instead of a period (sometimes called a *comma splice*)

sentence   a group of words expressing a complete thought; a statement

sequence   a given order of things, actions, events

subject   what a sentence is about; the *doer* or *doers* of the verb

support sentences   sentences used to develop and explain the idea introduced in the topic sentence

topic sentence   the sentence expressing the main idea of the paragraph

verb   the word that expresses action or helps to make a statement; the necessary word in every sentence

Organizing your writing

Any writing you do should have organization. Organization is how you present information. It involves the arrangement of your ideas and opinions. Part of organization deals with the order in which you present this information. Part of it deals with how you group your thoughts. Your ideas must be developed into sentences, then into paragraphs. Sometimes your paragraphs will have to be developed into essays or compositions. For example, you may have to write a research paper.

As you probably know, the sentence is the expression of a complete thought. Put simply, someone or something usually *does* something. An action occurs. An idea is expressed. Something *is* described. Pages 12-13 show you some basic sentence patterns. Now is the time to start improving your writing. Always read over what you have written. The material in this section will help you correct your errors.

Sentences do not stand alone. Sentences work together to form a paragraph. Paragraphs are a practical way of expressing your ideas in writing. You take statements that are related and put them in a logical order. To hold your ideas together you use a main sentence. This main sentence is the topic sentence.

TOPIC SENTENCES

The topic sentence is the key to writing a good paragraph. The topic sentence can appear anywhere in a paragraph. Most people place it in the first part of a paragraph. The topic sentence is usually the *first sentence*. It is the sentence that says *what* a paragraph is all about.

A topic sentence is more effective when it gives your attitude toward a topic. Read the topic sentences below. They appear in pairs labeled A and B. Both sentences in a pair are on the same topic. Which topic sentence in each pair is more effective—A or B?

A I spent my summer vacation in West Virginia.
B My summer vacation was an unforgettable adventure spent in the hills of wild, wonderful West Virginia.

A My room is on the second floor of our house.
B My room is a tiny loft-like retreat on the second floor of our house.

A My family owns an old upright piano.
B My family's old upright piano is the center of life in my house.

In each case, Sentence B is more effective. You learn about the topic as well as the writer's attitude toward the topic. For example, in Sentence A of the first example you do not learn what a vacation in West Virginia might be like. You are not told anything about the writer's opinion. But in Sentence B you get the writer's *impression* of a West Virginia vacation.

TOPIC vacationing in West Virginia
WRITER'S IMPRESSION an unforgettable adventure

Now you can read for the details, the sentences that support the topic sentence. The topic sentence, *My summer vacation was an unforgettable adventure spent in the hills of wild, wonderful West Virginia,* helps the writer *limit* what he or she will write about. You know that within the hills of West Virginia the writer had an exciting summer. As the reader, you now expect to share in those adventures.

Below are examples of topics and topic sentences. Notice how the topic sentence both *limits* the topic and states the opinion of the writer.

TOPIC	TOPIC SENTENCE
students in English 12	Everyone in Mr. Hamilton's English 12 class is intelligent, eager to learn, and creative.
my friend's character	Yesterday I realized that sincerity and loyalty are a significant part of my best friend's character.
high school sports	Baseball and soccer are especially good sports for high school students.

Activity 1

Analyzing topic sentences

Read the topic sentences below. First, find the topic. Then find the word or words that give the writer's opinion or attitude toward the topic.

EXAMPLE
Mrs. Marlow has the respect and admiration of all the students at Carl Sandburg High School.

Topic: Mrs. Marlow
Attitude: respect and admiration

1. I will always regret the day I disobeyed my father._____

2. My bedroom is the messiest room in our house._____

3. Everyone attending last night's game was physically and emotionally exhausted._____

4. Yesterday I discovered the value of real friendship._____

Activity 2

Writing better topic sentences

The sentences below are topic sentences. Some of these sentences need to have their topics *limited*. Some sentences need to include the writer's attitude or opinion. Other sentences need details to make the topic clear. *Rewrite* each of these topic sentences. Improve the sentences as you rewrite them.

EXAMPLE
I will never forget my summer vacation.

My summer vacation in Kentucky bluegrass country was the best vacation I have ever had.

1. I will never forget what happened last night.

_____

2. I will write about my best friend.

_____

3. I visited my grandmother last winter.

_____

4. My parents often tell me about life in Puerto Rico.

_____

5. On the plane I noticed several people staring at me.

_____

SUPPORT SENTENCES

After you have written a topic sentence that tells what the paragraph will be about, you will need to write some sentences that tell something about your topic. These sentences are support sentences. You will lose your reader's interest if you do not provide some details about your topic. These details are in sentences that support your topic sentence.

Here are some examples of topic sentences and sentences that support the topic.

TOPIC SENTENCE	DETAILS
I have a real fear of math exams.	• I feel shaky and cold when I take a math test. • Staying up all night to study before a math test doesn't help.
I would like to travel more.	• I have only traveled to two states outside of Ohio. • Once I visited relatives in Michigan and Kentucky.
I am trying hard to cut down on the time I spend watching television.	• I limit the time I watch TV to about 2 hours a day. • I watch one program after school and two programs at night.

Activity 3
Writing support sentences

Write at least two *support sentences* for each of the topic sentences below.

TOPIC SENTENCE	SUPPORT SENTENCES
My vacation in Florida was a real disaster.	_____ _____ _____ _____ _____
Inflation hurts all Americans, regardless of age, race, or income.	_____ _____ _____ _____ _____
My birthday is an exciting day for me.	_____ _____ _____ _____ _____

Activity 4
Evaluating writing

Read the following paragraph. Then answer the questions.

Sugar is bad for your health. When first eaten, it leaves you with a feeling of "quick energy." Very soon, however, the sugar level in your body goes down, leaving you feeling more tired than before. In addition, sugar is a leading cause of tooth decay, resulting in

6

discomfort and expense for millions of people. Then, too, sugar is high in calories. When used in large amounts, it can lead to a weight problem. As you can see, too much sugar in your diet can affect your health.

1. What is the topic sentence in this paragraph? _____
_____

2. What is the topic of this paragraph? _____
_____

3. Does the writer stick to this topic? Explain. _____
_____
_____

4. Are there at least three *support* sentences in this paragraph? _____

5. What words in the closing sentence go back to the topic and attitude expressed in the topic sentence?
_____

WRITING CONCLUSIONS

A good paragraph needs a closing sentence. A closing sentence tells the reader that you have expressed your ideas. It is the logical last statement. It is your conclusion. The conclusion should maintain the tone you have set and the point you have made.

In a one-paragraph paper you may be able to close effectively with just one sentence. But sometimes it takes two or three sentences to bring a report or composition to a close. In a longer paper you may even need an entire paragraph for the conclusion.

Here are some ideas to keep in mind when you write a closing sentence.

1. Bring the topic sentence to the reader's mind again. But you don't have to use the same words you used in the topic sentence.
2. Use transition words to help you conclude your thoughts: *consequently, therefore, then, in the same way.*
3. *Don't* contradict the point you have already made.
4. *Don't* start a new topic.
5. *Don't* apologize for what you didn't know or say.
6. *Don't* say that you are finished with statements like these:

    • And that's all I have to say on the subject.
    • And I hope you understand what I mean.
    • That's the end of my paragraph.
    • I hope you enjoyed this paper.
    • And so my closing sentence is . . . .

7. Be brief and clear.

Activity 5

Choosing a closing sentence

Below are three topic sentences. Opposite each sentence are three closing sentences. Which closing sentence fits the topic sentence best?

_____ 1. Mrs. Marlow has the respect and admiration of all the students at Carl Sandburg High School.

    a. Good teachers are hard to find.
    b. Mrs. Marlow has taught many students.
    c. Mrs. Marlow's hard work and fairness have earned the respect of all.

Explain. _____

_____

_____ 2. Our society must realize that drunk driving is a problem that must be solved.

    a. Drunk drivers are a menace to other people.
    b. As I have shown you in the above paragraph, this is a serious problem.
    c. Therefore, efforts to stop people from driving after drinking must be increased.

Explain. _____

_____

_____ 3. More students are dropping out of high school each year.

    a. However, many students are realizing the value of a high school diploma.
    b. Teachers should make school more enjoyable.
    c. Students must be forced to stay in high school until they graduate.

Explain. _____

_____

Activity 6

Writing topic sentences and paragraphs

Complete each of the following topic sentences. Then select one topic sentence and write your own paragraph. You can develop a paragraph in different ways. You can use _details, description,_ or _examples._ The paragraph you write must have:

- a topic sentence
- at least _three_ support sentences
- a closing sentence

Improve each of these topic sentences by adding words that express your own ideas or opinions.

EXAMPLE

I lose my temper whenever *someone asks me to do something which goes against my values.*

1. The first teacher I had taught me _____

2. My strongest personality trait is _____

3. My weakest personality trait is _____

4. The best movie I have ever seen is _____

5. As a teenager, I have learned to respect and admire _____

6. As a child, I feared _____

7. I am most sensitive in my dealings with people who _____

8. If there is one sport that I truly love, it is _____

9. My favorite celebrity is _____

10. The most compelling soap opera on TV is _____

Now write a paragraph using one of these sentences as the topic sentence.

Activity 7
Writing a paragraph

Select one of the topic sentences below. Develop the sentence into an effective paragraph. Be sure your paragraph has:

- a topic sentence
- at least five support sentences
- a concluding sentence

1. Last night on television I watched in amazement the birth of a baby.

2. My first day at _____ High School is a day I will long remember.

3. Corporations should be held responsible for polluting our air and water.

4. April Fool's Day is a fun day at my house.

5. Saint Patrick's Day is an important holiday in my family.

ORGANIZING YOUR SENTENCES IN TIME SEQUENCE

To express yourself clearly in writing, you must present your ideas in a logical order. This is an important part of being organized. The order of your ideas will depend on the type of writing you are doing.

Sometimes it is necessary to arrange your ideas in *time* order. You present details or events according to the order in which they happen. This arrangement is called chronological order. This arrangement is important. It will help you include the necessary details or events in a paragraph or paper.

Activity 8

Putting ideas in logical order

Read the paragraph below.

Air and fuel mixed in the combustion chamber catch fire. A jet engine works with only three basic parts: an air intake, a combustion chamber, and an exhaust outlet. First, air comes in through the air intake. The hot exploding gases push out at great speed through the exhaust outlet. The air and fuel mixture actually explodes in the chamber. As the gases push outward and backward, the plane moves forward.

Did this paragraph confuse you? The events described in the paragraph are out of order, or sequence. Rewrite the paragraph. Arrange the sentences in logical order. Use transitional words like *first, second, next* to help make the time sequence clear.

_____

_____

_____

_____

_____

_____

_____

_____

Activity 9

Expressing ideas in time sequence

Select one of the situations below. Write a paragraph arranging all your sentences in the correct order. Make up the necessary details for the situation you choose.

- You were involved in a minor automobile accident. You have to file an insurance claim. On the claim your insurance company asks you to *describe* the accident just as it happened.

_____

_____

_____

_____

_____

_____

_____

- You are one of TV's loyal soap opera fans. (Every afternoon you tune in to your favorite "soaps.") You are also a member of Ms. Green's basic writing class. Your class is discussing ways of organizing and improving student writing. Many students have trouble getting information down in a logical order. Students jump around from idea to idea and event to event. Ms. Green gives the class this assignment:

Write a paragraph describing the events that happened yesterday on your favorite soap opera. What happened first? . . . next? . . . and so forth. Use transitional words, *then, at this time, by now, finally,* etc., to help make the story clear to the class. Be sure your sentences are arranged in the correct time sequence.

_____

_____

_____

_____

_____

_____

_____

Coherent writing

What makes your writing coherent? What must you do to be sure a person can make sense of what you say? A number of skills are needed to produce coherent writing. One of these skills is using correct sentence patterns. For example, you would never say *John home went*. It is simply not a correct speech pattern in English.

SENTENCE PATTERNS

Your knowledge of the English language is probably greater than you realize. If you learned English as a child, you are considered a native speaker. You are already familiar with basic sentence patterns in the English language:

PATTERN 1	Subject	Verb	Adverb (optional)	
	The boy	walked	hurriedly.	
	First-graders	cry	easily.	
	I	went	home.	

PATTERN 2	Subject	Transitive Verb	Direct Object	
	Birds	eat	seeds.	
	The plumber	fixed	the sink.	
	I	want	the book.	

PATTERN 3	Subject	Transitive Verb	Indirect Object	Direct Object
	You	gave	the birds	the seeds.
	The plumber	gave	Mary	the bill.
	I	asked	Mary	a question.

PATTERN 4	Subject	Transitive Verb	Direct Object	Objective Complement
	Alex	called	me	a hero.
	They	elected	Shirley	chairperson.
	We	judged	him	guilty.

PATTERN 5	Subject	Linking Verb	Complement
	Pierre	is	French.
	Marva	was	angry.
	Reggie	acted	cool.
	Natalie	is	happy.
	Ronald	is	president.

Some verbs in English express action. These verbs can pass their action to objects. These verbs are called transitive.

I <u>gave</u> money. ┌—object

Raoul <u>shot</u> the basketball. ┌—object

Mr. Rivera <u>counted</u> the scorecards. ┌—object

Other verbs can also express action. But sometimes these verbs do not pass the action to an object. Verbs that express action without objects are called intransitive verbs.

I <u>ran.</u>
Raoul <u>arrived.</u>
Mr. Rivera <u>shouted.</u>

Still other verbs link, or join, the subject to a noun or adjective. These are linking verbs. The verb *to be* is an important linking verb. It is used to make statements that things *exist*. It has different forms to show different times, or tenses—past, present, or future. Here are some forms of the verb *to be*:

I am she.

Henry was angry.

Frank was sad.

Kelly will be a senior.

Here are other linking verbs.

I <u>felt</u> sad.
She <u>looked</u> happy.
Clark Kent <u>becomes</u> "Superman."
The food <u>smelled</u> delicious.

If you are a native speaker of English, these patterns come naturally to you. If you are not a native speaker, become familiar with the basic sentence patterns. Know which verbs can take objects and which verbs cannot. You must use the right sentence pattern and the right type of verb if your writing is to be coherent.

Activity 10

Using basic sentence patterns

Fill in a word or phrase that will complete each of the sentence patterns below.

1. I went _____ in a rush.

2. Paula and Betty felt _____ about trying to trick me.

3. Mary White was _____ president of the class.

4. We voted _____ president.

5. My father gave the _____ a bath.

6. Mother offered _____ a _____ .

7. Sylvia is _____ .

8. My name is _____ .

9. My mother's maiden name is _____ .

10. Dogs eat meat and _____ .

11. They ran _____ .

12. The woman arrived _____ .

FORMING SENTENCES

A sentence is the expression of a complete thought. It is a statement. It *always* has a subject and a verb. Sometimes the verb is more than one word. When the verb is more than one word, it is called a *verb phrase*.

Subject ⌐   ⌐──── Verb
        She ran away.
Subject ⌐   ⌐──── Verb phrase
        She has run away.

The subject is the person performing the action, or the *doer*, and the verb is the *action word*. The verb expresses *what happened*. The verb also tells you *when* something happened.

Here are examples of the four types of sentences you will use in your writing.

1. The simple sentence: He drove to the airport.

   - This sentence contains a subject and a verb. The subject and verb together make up a *clause.*
   - The clause can stand alone and make sense. It is *independent.*

2. The compound sentence: He drove to the airport, but he missed his plane.

   - This sentence contains two *clauses:*

     He drove to the airport
     He missed his plane

   - Each clause can stand alone and still make sense.
   - Clauses like these may be connected by *and, but,* or *or.*

3. The complex sentence: He drove to the airport although he was very tired.

   - This sentence contains two *clauses:*

     He drove to the airport
     although he was very tired

   - One clause can stand alone and still make sense:

     He drove to the airport.

   - The other clause cannot stand alone and make sense:

     although he was very tired

   - A word like *when, where, although, because,* or *while* is used at the beginning of the clause that is *dependent*:

     although he was very tired

   - A dependent clause cannot stand alone. It does not make sense by itself.

4. The compound-complex sentence: He drove to the airport, but he missed his plane because he forgot to take his ticket.

   - This sentence contains two *independent clauses*:

     He drove to the airport
     he missed his plane

   - The clauses are joined by *but,* and each clause can stand alone and still make sense.

- BUT there is a third clause:

  because <u>he</u> <u>forgot</u> his ticket

- This clause cannot stand alone. It does not make sense without <u>he missed his plane.</u>
- This clause begins with the word *because*. It is the dependent clause, or the *complex* part of a compound-complex sentence.

Improving sentences

Writing is hardly ever perfect the first time. Make it a habit to look over what you have written. Change words or phrases. Rearrange sentences. Correct mistakes. Always try to improve your writing.

RUN-ON SENTENCES

Student writers sometimes find it hard to identify sentences. These writers may combine two sentences into one. They use the wrong punctuation or no punctuation at all. The result is a run-on sentence.

RUN-ON: I opened the door the salesman walked in.
CORRECTION: I opened the door. The salesman walked in.
> *OR*
> I opened the door, and the salesman walked in.

RUN-ON: We studied hard for the exam however our notes were not detailed enough.
CORRECTION: We studied hard for the exam. However, our notes were not detailed enough.
> *OR*
> We studied hard for the exam; however, our notes were not detailed enough.
> *Note.* A semicolon must be used with words like *however, consequently, therefore,* and *nevertheless* in a sentence with two independent clauses.

In this run-on sentence the writer uses a comma where a period belongs.

RUN-ON: I enjoy walking on the beach, it is very relaxing.
CORRECTION: I enjoy walking on the beach. It is very relaxing.

SENTENCE FRAGMENTS

A fragment is a part of a sentence. A fragment may be a clause and have both a subject and a verb. But it may still not be able to stand alone. A fragment should not be punctuated as if it were a sentence.

FRAGMENTS: Because you are my friend
While I was in North Dakota
When I go to a rock concert
During the year that I was away
Although I like you

A phrase may contain an *ing* word, but it still does not mean it can stand alone.

FRAGMENTS: Running down the hill
Sending the wire
Helping people who are in trouble
The girl wearing the Wonder Woman costume

Seeing a verb form often makes students think they see a sentence.

FRAGMENTS: Dressed as Spider Man.
To run a good race.
To have gone without food.
Just to be able to dance.

Activity 11   Correct these run-on sentences.

Correcting run-ons and fragments

1. Roy found the missing part, it was still in the box.

_____

2. Sally told us the score we could not believe it.

_____

3. Mrs. Hill came in the classroom frowning she had graded our midterm tests.

_____

4. Ellen exercised for over two hours, she wanted to lose weight in a hurry.

_____

5. I ran to answer the phone my brother sat waiting my sister kept reading her book everybody in the room wanted me to answer the telephone.

_____

_____

_____

Make these fragments complete sentences.

1. down the hill and around the corner

_____

2. just to be able to play my tape recorder

_____

3. running through the crowded streets

_____

4. knowing how my mother hates for me to be late for dinner

_____

5. to stay healthy and trim

_____

Verbs

Using verbs correctly is important to improving sentences. You should know that most verbs add -s to the third person singular verb form in the present tense.

EXAMPLE:

	Singular	**Plural**
First person	I like pizza.	We like pizza.
Second person	You like pizza.	You like pizza.
Third person	She likes pizza.	They like pizza.
	He likes pizza.	

Most verbs add -d or -ed to show the past tense.

EXAMPLES:
I walked home alone.
The children liked playing at the beach.

Many common verbs, however, do not follow this rule. These are called *irregular* verbs. These verb forms have to be memorized because each one is different. Here are a few of the most common irregular verbs for you to study.

IRREGULAR VERBS

Basic Form	Past	Past Participle (with *has, have,* or *had*)
begin	began	begun
blow	blew	blown
break	broke	broken
choose	chose	chosen
come	came	come
do	did	done
draw	drew	drawn
drive	drove	driven
eat	ate	eaten
give	gave	given
go	went	gone
have	had	had
know	knew	known
run	ran	run
see	saw	seen
steal	stole	stolen
swim	swam	swum
tear	tore	torn
throw	threw	thrown
write	wrote	written

Be is a special verb. It has many forms that are important to learn. In the present tense, *be* has three forms: *am, are,* and *is.*

EXAMPLE:

	Singular	**Plural**
First person	I am.	We are.
Second person	You are.	You are.
Third person	He is. She is. It is.	They are.

In the past tense, *be* has two forms: *was* and *were.*

EXAMPLE:

	Singular	**Plural**
First person	I was.	We were.
Second person	You were.	You were.
Third person	She was. He was. It was.	They were.

Activity 12

Using the correct verb form

Select the correct verb form in each of the following sentences.

1. (Are, Be) you going to the beach today? _____

2. Jim (is, am) going to the movies. _____

3. The team (is, be) happy about winning the game. _____

4. You (were, was) gone when I got to your house. _____

5. (Was, Were) you pleased with your grade? _____

6. Sally (play, plays) the piano. _____

7. He (like, likes) the football coach. _____

8. The teacher (wants, want) everyone to be quiet. _____

9. Jim (try, tries) hard to be a good student. _____

10. It (look, looks) like rain. _____

TENSE SHIFTS

A common error in writing is to shift verb tenses. The tense of all verbs in a piece of writing should usually be the same. Proofread your writing. Check all the verbs to be sure they express the right time period. The paragraph below illustrates the tense shift error. The verbs in each sentence are underlined.

> In the morning, Beverly takes a subway uptown to work. Then she went to her job in a tall office building on 58th Street. She talks with her boss for a few minutes. Then she goes to her own office. There Beverly planned her work for the day.

Here is the paragraph with the tense shift corrected.

> In the morning, Beverly takes a subway uptown to work. Then she goes to her job in a tall office building on 58th Street. She talks with her boss for a few minutes. Then she goes to her own office. There Beverly plans her work for the day.

Sometimes you *have to* change tense to make your meaning clear. Remember that tense shows the time of an action. Do not shift back and forth in time unless it is necessary. If you change from present to past to present again, you will confuse the time period in the reader's mind. Avoid tense shifts within a sentence, within a series of sentences, or within a series of paragraphs.

Activity 13

Correcting tense shifts

Rewrite each sentence. Correct the tense shifts in each sentence. Make your tense corrections agree with the first verb in each sentence.

EXAMPLE:
When I looked in his direction, he looks the other way.

When I looked in his direction, he looked the other way.

1. She took a cab downtown, and gets out at my apartment.

   _____

2. I told him that the store was closing, but he comes in anyway.

   _____

3. The teacher presented the basic format, and then she has the students fill in the details.

   _____

4. He gave an excellent performance as Othello; he really seems to have gotten into the part.

   _____

5. The instructor came into the room, gives us a lecture, and then passed out our test papers.

   _____

TENSE AND SUBJECT-VERB AGREEMENT ERRORS

Some errors in writing are the result of informal speaking. For example, some people do not always say clearly the -d or -ed of verbs in the past tense. Others do not use the third person -s to show agreement in the present tense. They might *say,* "He like it." or "She write good letters." Transferring this kind of speaking to writing causes problems.

Activity 14

Correcting verb errors

Check your tense and agreement skills. Then look at page 18 for some examples to help you. Fill in the correct verb form in each of the sentences below. Add -d or -ed to show past time (tense). Add -s to make the third person singular (he, she, or it) agree with the verb in the present tense. If the verb *do* or *have* is used in the present tense, do you know how to show third person agreement? How should you spell *do*? How should you spell *have*?

PRESENT   **1.** Joseph _____ crazy when he goes on stage.
                         go

PAST   **2.** My Aunt Alice _____ the incident to me.
                                relate

PAST   **3.** Albert _____ the baby's diaper.
                           change

PAST   **4.** Yesterday I _____ for sunshine and got it.
                         wish

PRESENT	**5.** Simon _____ sausage and eggs. like	
PAST	**6.** He _____ the stairs slowly. climb	
PAST	**7.** We _____ the problem at the last meeting. discuss	
PRESENT	**8.** Chester _____ us with his great "one-liners." amuse	
PAST	**9.** She _____ several questions of the professor. ask	
PAST	**10.** He _____ to play tennis on Saturdays. use	

Punctuation END MARKS FOR SENTENCES

A sentence must have a punctuation mark at the end. Most sentences end with a *period.* Questions should always end with a *question mark.* Use an *exclamation mark* after a sentence that shows strong feeling.

EXAMPLES:
Statement: She went home.
Question: Did she go home?
Exclamation: Go home right now!

COMMAS IN SENTENCES

1. The two clauses of compound sentences are separated by a comma. Remember that each clause can stand alone and still make sense.

   EXAMPLES:
   She went home, and she carried all her books with her.
   John is a good student, and he is also a fine athlete.

2. The complex sentence uses a comma to separate clauses *when the dependent clause comes first.* Remember, a dependent clause cannot stand alone and still make sense:

   Because I feel tired, I'm going to lie down.
   When Tanya is ready, we'll go to a movie.

   If the dependent clause comes after the independent clause, you *do not* need a comma:

   I'm going to lie down because I'm tired.
   We'll go to a movie when Tanya is ready.

3. The compound-complex sentence should be punctuated as follows:

   Because I'm tired, I will lie down, but I won't fall asleep.

   • The first comma separates the independent and dependent clauses when the dependent clause comes first.
   • The second comma separates two independent clauses joined by *but.*

She bought a book at the book store, and she bought some flowers while she was in the flower shop.

- The comma separates two independent clauses joined by *and*.
- No comma is necessary after the word *flowers* because the dependent clause comes at the end of the sentence.

OTHER USES OF COMMAS

1. Use commas to separate items in a series. Do not use a comma after the last item.

   EXAMPLES:
   Jim, David, Lisa, and Angela went to the movies.
   You should take books, paper, pencils, and an assignment notebook to every class.

2. Use a comma between the day of the week and the date. Use a comma between the date and the year.

   EXAMPLES:
   Pearl Harbor was attacked on Sunday, December 7, 1941.
   I was born on June 9, 1968.

3. Use a comma after introductory words like *well, yes,* and *no.*

   EXAMPLES:
   No, I don't want to go to the game.
   Well, you really tried hard on the test.

4. Use a comma around words that interrupt a sentence.

   EXAMPLES:
   The story, however, is true.
   Their trip, consequently, had to be delayed.

Activity 15

Using end marks and commas

Rewrite the following sentences. Use end marks and commas correctly in each sentence.

1. Jane please come home with us

_____

2. Do you like playing soccer

_____

3. Watch out

_____

4. I bought hamburgers potato chips and cokes

_____

5. Joe likes football but he dislikes baseball

_____

6. Although sports programs for girls are new in some schools the teams have done well.

_____

7. Because it was raining the game was cancelled

_____

8. No I don't like jogging

_____

9. Tina likes her new job but the hours are too long

_____

10. M*A*S*H was on TV for eleven years and the reruns will be on for a few more years

_____

Capitalization

Using capital letters correctly is important in your writing. Here are the basic rules for capital letters.

1. Use a capital letter to begin each sentence.

   EXAMPLES:
   Here are your shoes.
   Today is my birthday.

2. Always capitalize the pronoun I.

   EXAMPLES:
   Dad and I like to take long walks.
   He and I went to a movie.

3. Use capitals for the *names* of specific person, places, or things.

   EXAMPLES:
   New York City   Nichols Middle School
   Chevrolet   France
   Jon Walters   Civic Center

4. Capitalize the first and last words and all important words in titles.

   EXAMPLES:
   Book   *The Outsiders*
   Magazine   *Road and Track*
   Record Album   *Concert in Central Park*

Song   "Take the A Train"
Movie   *An Officer and a Gentleman*
TV Show   "Days of Our Lives"

5. Capitalize the names of religions, nationalities, and races.

   EXAMPLES:
   They belong to the Protestant, Catholic, or Jewish faiths.
   Last night we had Mexican food.
   Who are the real Native Americans?

6. Capitalize the name of a family relationship when it is used with a person's name. Do not capitalize the name of a family relationship when it is not used with a person's name.

   EXAMPLES:
   I want you to meet my Aunt Bessie.
   My aunt is coming next week.

Activity 16
Using capital letters

Copy each of the following sentences. Put capital letters where they belong.

1. I really enjoyed the book, *anatomy of a murder*.

   _____

2. My aunt ruth took me to a french restaurant with my cousins.

   _____

3. Is austin a large city?

   _____

4. I always enjoy our family picnic at greenland national park.

   _____

5. The song "remember my name" is a top seller.

   _____

Words commonly confused

When you speak, no one knows if you are saying "it's" or "its" for *it is*. But "it's" and "its" have two different meanings. If you write the wrong word, the reader may get confused or think you are not very smart. And seeing the wrong word is distracting. The words listed here are words people confuse the most often. These words either sound alike or have almost the same spelling. Study these words and their meanings. Then complete Activity 17.

accept   to take something that is offered
  I accept your gift.

except   not including, leaving out
  Everyone was invited except me.

already   by that time, previously
  We had already seen the show.

all ready   everyone ready, all prepared
  When you are all ready, we will go.

altogether   completely, entirely
  You are altogether correct.

all together   everyone together in the same place
  We were all together for the celebration.

alright   a wrong spelling of *all right*

all right   correct form
  Is going to a movie all right with you?

capital   a chief city, money, an upper-case letter
  Washington, D.C. is the capital of the United States.
  Put your capital in the bank.
  Use a capital letter.

capitol   a building where a law-making body meets
  We visited the Capitol in Washington.

council   a group that makes decisions
  She is a member of the City Council.

counsel   advise, to give advice
  I need someone to counsel me.

desert   dry land; to leave or abandon
  He rode across the desert.
  Do not desert me.

dessert   final course of a meal
  I enjoyed the fancy dessert.

its   possessive
  The cat licked its paws.

it's   contraction of *it is*
  It's very cold today.

lead   to go in front (present tense)
You should lead us.

led   to go in front (past tense)
He led the parade.

lead   a heavy metal
The box is made of lead.

loose   free, not tight
The belt feels loose.

lose   to misplace
Did you lose your keys?

peace   absence of war
We all want world peace.

piece   part of something
I'd like a piece of cake.

passed   to go by
I passed Joe's house.

past   time gone by
I like to think about past vacations.

principal   head of a school; most important
She is our principal.
The principal reason for mistakes is carelessness.

principle   rule, belief
The principle of solar energy is clear.

stationary   standing in one position
The train is stationary.

stationery   writing paper
Buy some stationery at the store.

there   in that place
Put the book over there.

their   belonging to them
It is their car.

they're   contraction of *they are*
They're ready to leave.

to   preposition
Give the books to me.

too   also
You may go, too.

two   number
He has two brothers.

who's   contraction of *who is* or *who has*
Who's your friend? Who's lost a dollar?

whose   possessive
Whose jacket is this?

your   possessive
Is that your coat?

you're   contraction of *you are*
You're very busy today.

Activity 17   Select the right word for each sentence.

Selecting the right word

1. My friend was able to _____ me.
(council/counsel)

2. The _____ of our school is also an experienced teacher.
(principal/principle)

3. We had chocolate cake for _____ .
(desert/dessert)

4. I am so glad I _____ the exam.
(past/passed)

5. I hope I don't _____ my gloves.
(lose/loose)

6. We took the books _____ the library.
(to/too)

7. _____ got the money?
(Who's/Whose)

8. The evening star is almost _____ .
(stationery/stationary)

9. The business failed because there was not enough _____ .
(capital/capitol)

10. _____ certain to rain the day of the school parade.
(Its/It's)

11. I hope he will _____ your first offer.
(except/accept)

12. I am not _____ pleased with Paul's behavior.
　　　　　　　(altogether/all together)

13. I hope it is _____ for me to be here.
　　　　　　　　(alright/all right)

14. _____ always on time for work.
　　(Their/They're)

15. Please put the box over _____ .
　　　　　　　　　　(their/there)

16. Please pass me a _____ of pie.
　　　　　　　　(peace/piece)

17. He _____ the marching band.
　　　　(lead/led)

18. I have _____ seen that movie.
　　　　　　(all ready/already)

19. I hope you can learn to drive, _____ .
　　　　　　　　　　　　(too/to)

20. Please let me know if _____ not going.
　　　　　　　　(your/you're)

Editing your writing

Certain errors often appear in student writing. You might see run-on sentences and fragments. There may be errors in choosing tenses. There may be verb form errors, especially with irregular verbs. Always proofread your writing. Pay special attention to these errors and errors in *subject-verb agreement, capitalization,* and *punctuation.* (Many mistakes in punctuation are comma errors.) Always correct these mistakes. Be sure your writing is clear and easy for others to read.

The activities that follow will help you to discover what you know about *subject-verb agreement, capitalization,* and *punctuation.*

Activity 18

Subject-verb agreement

Subject-verb agreement problems occur in both written and oral communications. The third-person singular agreement error occurs most often. Select what *your* verb choice would be in each of the sentences below. Remember, singular subjects take an *-s* in the third person present. The third person is *he, she,* or *it.* If you find it hard to identify the subjects, find the verb first. Then ask *who* or *what* performed the action expressed by the verb.

1. Cindy (live/lives) next door to me. _____

2. The subject of the speech (was/were) new taxes. _____

3. (Don't/Doesn't) Elise wear her hair in braids? _____

4. Anne (has/have) her books with her. _____

5. There (is/are) plenty of seats in the auditorium. _____

6. Everything in the store (is/are) on sale. _____

7. It (look/looks) like rain. _____

8. I (give/gave) fifty dollars to the church. _____

9. He (is/be) angry with me. _____

10. There (is/are) my boss and his friend. _____

11. He (carry/carried) the box up the stairs. _____

12. They (was/were) happy about the new computer center. _____

13. The team (have/has) won their last six games. _____

14. I (do/does) want an after-school job. _____

15. It (is/are) a long walk to the game arcade. _____

16. Angela (like/likes) jumping rope. _____

17. I (don't/doesn't) like this dress. _____

18. The car (stop/stopped) in the middle of traffic. _____

19. The newspaper (sell/sells) for fifty cents. _____

20. It (is/be) important to learn to cook. _____

Activity 19
Editing for commas

Read the following sentences carefully. Copy each sentence and insert commas where they belong.

1. No we shouldn't complain.

_____

2. When all the children are ready we can start the game.

_____

3. We searched for pennies nickels and dimes in the sand.

_____

4. The damage to the building however was less than we thought.

_____

5. It snowed all day and the airport was closed.

_____

6. Joe likes bike riding swimming and baseball in the summer.

_____

7. I am not happy with my job but I don't want to quit.

_____

8. The meeting was held on Wednesday March 9 1970.

_____

9. Although they practiced hard the team was not ready for the game.

_____

10. I am good at math and I also like science.

_____

Activity 20

Editing for capitalization

Copy each of the following sentences. Add capitals where they are needed. You will also need to take out capitals that are wrong.

1. I have always wanted to visit new york city.

_____

2. The amazon river is very long.

_____

3. My parakeet likes seeds and Lettuce.

_____

4. Do you like Chinese Food?

_____

5. The afro-american construction company has the contract for the new building.

_____

6. I enjoyed the book called a wind in the door.

_____

7. My favorite tv program is As The World Turns.

_____

8. How many german restaurants can you name?

_____

9. I like to listen to my Aunt Liz and my Cousins talking.

_____

10. They lived on Elmwood Avenue last Year.

_____

PROOFREADER'S CHECKLIST

Organization
- Does your paragraph have a topic sentence?
- Did you write support sentences to make your paragraph complete?
- Do you have a closing sentence?
- Are your sentences arranged in a logical order? Does your writing require arrangement in time sequence? If so, have you put your sentences in time order?

Coherence
- Have you used correct sentence patterns?
- Do any of your sentences sound awkward? Do they need to be rewritten?
- Did you make the correct word choices? Check your dictionary if you are not certain of the word you should use.
- Did you use the correct part of speech?
- Have you checked for fragments and run-ons?
- Have you checked spelling?
- Have you accidentally left out a necessary word? You can use a caret (∧) to insert a missing word.
- Did you avoid any shifting of tenses?

Grammar & Punctuation
- Do all subjects and verbs agree in number? In the present tense, plural subjects take plural verbs. But watch for the third person singular. Third person singular subjects need -s added to the verb.
- Do you have all the necessary punctuation marks?
- Do all sentences begin with a capital letter?
- Do all sentences have an end punctuation mark?
- Have you shown all -d and -ed endings on past tense verbs?
- Have you used all _irregular_ verbs correctly?

CHECK YOUR UNDERSTANDING OF BASIC WRITING

1. Write a paragraph on any topic you choose. Be sure you have a topic sentence, three to five support sentences, and a conclusion sentence. When you have finished writing your paragraph, proofread it. Use the Proofreader's Checklist on page 32 to check organization, coherence, grammar, and punctuation. Rewrite if necessary.

2. The news stories below have been revised. There are now *five* errors in each. Can you identify these errors? Choose one of these news stories and proofread for errors. Rewrite the paragraph correcting the errors.

Two Woodlawn teenagers recieved medals for heroism at a special program at City Hall yesterday.

Alderman Robert W. Birch presented the medals to David C. Harvey and Nathan D. Weisberger, both sophmores at Lake Shore, High School.

"These boys are definately examples of the kind of citizens our nation needs," Birch said. "They risked there lives to rescue a drowning girl."

Spelling errors — 3
Punctuation — 1
Wrong Word — 1

The West Side Raiders raced to their third victory in a row last night and sank the East Side Vikings 27-10.

The 150th career victory for Mr. Greg Harvey, coach of the Raiders.

From the opening kickoff it was clear that the Raiders would win. Bruce Ross returns the ball to the Viking 35-yard line. Two plays later, George Harris race into the end zone for the first score.

In the second Quarter, Harris again ran with the ball. He take a Duane Hilliard pass into the end zone for the third TD of the game.

Capitalization Error — 1
Tense Shift — 1
Subject-Verb Agreement — 2
Fragment — 1

Writing letters and personal memos

Many important communications are in writing. One of the most important everyday writing skills is letter writing. In this section you will practice writing letters. You will write both personal and business letters. A well-written letter may be part of your job search. You may want to write your senator about a new law up for a vote. You may have to write for information to do a term paper. There are a number of occasions that require good letter writing skills. This section also discusses the personal memo. Do you know what a personal memo is? Have you ever written one? Effective personal memos require both listening and writing skills. Writing Letters and Memos gives you real life application of many of the writing skills you reviewed in the section called Basic Writing. A special section on consumer complaints follows this section. It deals with both telephone and written complaints. Again, you will put your letter-writing skills to use.

Writing letters

WORDS TO KNOW

closing   the ending of a letter, such as "Sincerely yours," or "Cordially,"

correspondence   communication by writing or sending letters; the letters themselves

destination address   the name and location of the person or organization to whom a letter is addressed

heading   the letter writer's address and date placed at the beginning of a letter

inside address   the address of the person to whom a letter is written placed before the salutation

return address   the letter writer's address placed at the top left corner of the envelope

salutation   the greeting, such as "Dear . . .," placed below the inside address

ZIP Code   Zone Improvement Plan, a five digit number used by the U.S. Postal Service to help sort and distribute mail

ZIP + 4   the old postal ZIP Code plus four new numbers

The personal letter

Have you ever written a personal letter? If so, did you know the right form? Have you ever written a business letter? There is a special form that business letters should follow. After you wrote your letter, did you address the envelope? Did you use ZIP Codes and state abbreviations correctly? And did your letter reach the person you wanted to reach?

Many Americans do not know how to write letters or address envelopes correctly. Before you start to practice these skills, study the terms under *Words to Know.*

The personal letter is one that you write to friends or relatives. It has five parts: the heading, the salutation, the body, the closing, and the signature.

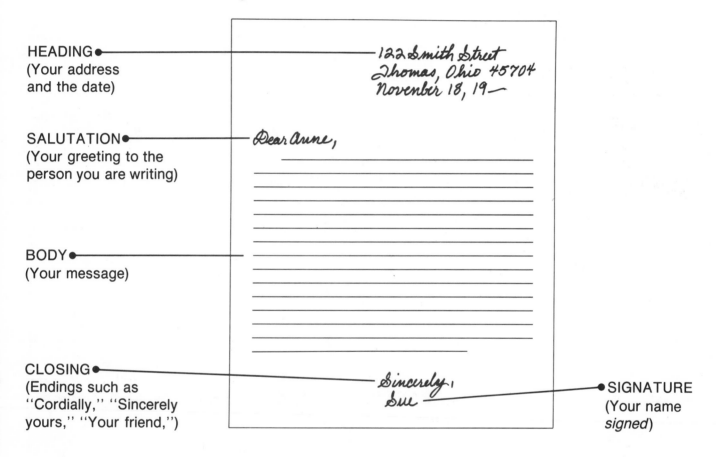

HEADING
(Your address
and the date)

SALUTATION
(Your greeting to the
person you are writing)

BODY
(Your message)

CLOSING
(Endings such as
"Cordially," "Sincerely
yours," "Your friend,")

SIGNATURE
(Your name
signed)

122 Smith Street
Thomas, Ohio 45704
November 18, 19—

Dear Anne,

Sincerely,
Sue

Most personal letters will be written just to keep in touch. They will be written to close friends and relatives. However, sometime you may write other types of personal letters.

One type of personal letter you need to write is the letter of thanks. You may wish to thank someone for a gift. You may want to thank someone for inviting you to be a week end guest. A letter of thanks can create good will toward you.

If you write a letter of thanks, be sure to mention the specific gift or visit. These details help to show that you appreciate what was done for you. If you were given a gift, you may have already used it or worn it. You can mention this in your letter. It should please the person who receives the letter.

Activity 1
Personal letters of thanks

Study the following letter of thanks. Notice that it is short. Also notice that the letter is very specific. Use this letter as a model to write your own letter of thanks. Think of a gift you have received. Or think of something someone has done for you. Then write your letter.

> 1304 Elmwood
> Park Ridge, IL
> March 27, 19—
>
> Dear Aunt Georgia and Uncle Henry,
> Thank you so much for the portable radio with headphones. It made a great birthday present.
> I really do like the headphones. Now I can listen to my favorite music when I go jogging. Yesterday, I took the radio with me on a long bike ride. My friends all tell me they want a radio just like mine.
>
> Love,
> John

Activity 2
Writing a personal letter

Pretend that your favorite sports star or actor is a good friend of yours. Write a letter to your friend. Tell him or her how much you enjoyed a recent television performance. Look at the sample personal letter on the opposite page. It will give you the correct form.

Activity 3
Writing a letter of invitation

Write a letter of invitation to a friend. Ask your friend to a party at your house. Make up the time and date of the party. Remember to answer the questions who, what, when, where, and why in your letter. Read the finished letter aloud to someone else. Ask that person to repeat the facts of the invitation to you. Have you put in all the necessary details? Have you remembered the five parts of a personal letter?

The business letter

A business letter has six parts: the heading, the inside address, the salutation, the body, the closing, and the signature. The part included in a business letter that is not in a personal letter is the *inside address*. The inside address gives the name and address of the person you are writing. Including this information gives you a complete record of your correspondence. The inside address is a necessary part of a business letter. *It appears just before the salutation.*

HEADING
(Your address and the date)

122 Smith Street
Thomas, Ohio 45706
November 18, 19___

INSIDE ADDRESS
(Address of the person or business you are writing)

Mr. Peter Kells
Personnel Manager
Mill Mart Company
1378 Fulton Drive
Lakeside, Kansas 66043

SALUTATION
(Your greeting to the person you are writing)

Dear Sir:

BODY
(Your message)

CLOSING
(Ending such as "Cordially," "Sincerely," etc.)

Sincerely yours,

Susan Wright

SIGNATURE
(Your name typed and *signed*)

Susan Wright

Keep these things in mind when writing a business letter:
1. Never forget to put the *date* in your heading. You may need to refer to it at another time. Make a copy of important letters.
2. Again, the *inside address* gives you the name of the person to whom you sent your letter. When you do not have the name of a specific person, use a title or department.

Director of Customer Complaints
Mill Mart Company
1328 Fulton Drive
Lakeside, Kansas 66043

Mill Mart Company
Frozen Foods Division
1328 Fulton Drive
Lakeside, Kansas 66043

3. The *salutation* is followed by a colon (:). Some examples of salutations are:

Dear Sir:	Dear Ms. Johnson:
Dear Sirs:	Dear Mr. Kelly:
Dear Madam:	Dear Student (Customer, Client, etc.):

4. The body of a business letter carries your message. Say what you have to say clearly. Keep your letter as short as possible.

5. Some typical closings are:

Yours truly,	Cordially yours,
Very truly yours,	Respectfully yours,
Sincerely,	

Notice that only the *first* letter of these closings is capitalized. A *comma* comes after the closing.

6. If your letter is handwritten, write your *signature* neatly. If you type a business letter, you still must sign your name. Type the closing and your name. Leave enough space between the closing and your name for your signature.

Sincerely yours,

Susan Wright

Susan Wright

The letter you will write to apply for a job is called the letter of application. It will follow the same form as the business letters you study here.

Activity 4

Writing a business letter

On your own paper, write a business letter. Use one of the choices below. If you do not know an address, check your telephone directory. You can also check product labels or bills you have received.

a. Write a business letter to the manufacturer of a product you like (or dislike). Explain why you use (or stopped using) the product.

b. Write a letter to a nonprofit organization (religious organization, library volunteers, tutoring services, neighborhood groups, etc.) offering your time and services. Be sure you let them know when and how to contact you.

c. Write a letter to one of the companies listed below. Explain that you wish to cancel your membership:

The Bookworm Club	CAMCASS Record & Tape Club	Liberty Magazine
888 8th Avenue	106 S. Martin Street	1520 Park Avenue
Newport, Indiana 47966	Mainland, Ohio 44057	Evansville, Maine 04106

Addressing envelopes

Writing the address on the envelope for your personal and business letter is just as important as writing the letter. If the address is written correctly, it means that your letter will get where you want it to go.

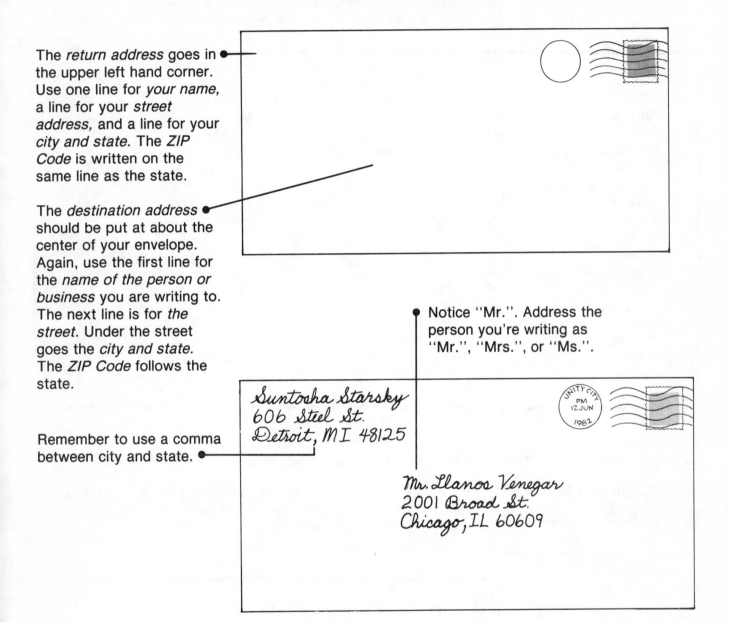

The *return address* goes in the upper left hand corner. Use one line for *your name,* a line for your *street address,* and a line for your *city and state.* The *ZIP Code* is written on the same line as the state.

The *destination address* should be put at about the center of your envelope. Again, use the first line for the *name of the person or business* you are writing to. The next line is for *the street.* Under the street goes the *city and state.* The *ZIP Code* follows the state.

Remember to use a comma between city and state.

Notice "Mr.". Address the person you're writing as "Mr.", "Mrs.", or "Ms.".

Suntosha Starsky
606 Steel St.
Detroit, MI 48125

Mr. Llanos Venegar
2001 Broad St.
Chicago, IL 60609

When addressing an envelope, remember to capitalize all proper nouns. A proper noun names a particular person, place, or thing. Look at the envelope above again. Notice that the sender's name is capitalized—Suntosha Starkey. Notice that the name of the person receiving this letter is capitalized—Mr. Llanos Venegar. And because "Steel" and "Broad" name particular streets, they are capitalized. What about "Detroit, MI" and "Chicago, IL"? Why are they capitalized?

State abbreviations

If you had to abbreviate *Arkansas,* would you write *Ark.* or *AR?* Both abbreviations are correct. *Ark.* is the traditional abbreviation for Arkansas. *AR* is the new two-letter abbreviation. The U.S. Postal Service now suggests we use these two-letter abbreviations. These abbreviations are written with capital letters and no periods.

Alabama .... AL	Kentucky .... KY	Ohio .... OH
Alaska .... AK	Louisiana .... LA	Oklahoma .... OK
Arizona .... AZ	Maine........................... ME	Oregon .... OR
Arkansas .... AR	Maryland...................... MD	Pennsylvania................ PA
California .... CA	Massachusetts .... MA	Puerto Rico................... PR
Colorado....................... CO	Michigan....................... MI	Rhode Island .... RI
Connecticut.................. CT	Minnesota.................... MN	South Carolina.............. SC
Delaware .... DE	Mississippi .... MS	South Dakota .... SD
District of Columbia....... DC	Missouri .... MO	Tennessee.................... TN
Florida .... FL	Montana .... MT	Texas .... TX
Georgia .... GA	Nebraska...................... NE	Utah............................. UT
Guam........................... GU	Nevada......................... NV	Vermont....................... VT
Hawaii.......................... HI	New Hampshire............. NH	Virginia .... VA
Idaho .... ID	New Jersey .... NJ	Virgin Islands................ VI
Illinois.......................... IL	New Mexico.................. NM	Washington .... WA
Indiana......................... IN	New York...................... NY	West Virginia .... WV
Iowa............................. IA	North Carolina .... NC	Wisconsin .... WI
Kansas .... KS	North Dakota................ ND	Wyoming .... WY

Common address abbreviations

Here is a list of common address abbreviations. Businesses using automatic addressing machines use these abbreviations. These abbreviations use no periods. Only capital letters are used.

Avenue ....AVE	Meadows ...MDWS	Shore ....SH
East .... E	North................. N	South .... S
Expressway .EXPY	Palms .... PLMS	Square ....SQ
Heights ....HTS	Park ....PK	Station ....STA
Hospital.......HOSP	Parkway ....PKY	Terrace ....TER
Institute........INST	Plaza..............PLZ	Turnpike.......TPKE
Junction ....JCT	Ridge ....RDG	Union ....UN
Lake................LK	River ....RV	View................VW
Lakes.............LKS	Road...............RD	Village...........VLG
Lane................LN	Rural .... R	West .... W

40

ZIP stands for Zone Improvement Plan. You should use the ZIP Code on your mail. Its use will help your letter get where you want it to go. Write your ZIP Code on forms that you fill out, too. It will help your return mail get to you quickly. The ZIP Code is a number that identifies areas in the United States. It helps the Postal Service sort and distribute mail. The correct ZIP Code should be part of the destination address. It should appear on the last line. There should also be a ZIP Code in the return address. Each ZIP Code should follow the name of the state.

ZIP + 4 is a new type of ZIP Code. It lets the Postal Service make better use of machines to sort first-class letters. ZIP + 4 is a voluntary program, like the use of ZIP Codes. If you want your letter to reach the proper address quickly, though, you will include the proper ZIP Code. The nine-digit ZIP + 4 number includes your old ZIP Code plus four new numbers. The new numbers allow the Postal Service to sort mail by small areas. Mail can be sorted by one side of a city block or both sides of a particular street. Mail can even be sorted by one floor of a large building. The Postal Service hopes that all persons will eventually use the new ZIP + 4 numbers.

Activity 5

Addressing envelopes

Study the samples below. Which sample would reach its destination without any difficulty? The letter is from Elvina Allen, 421 Wonder Lane, Blossom, MI 48106. It is going to Margo Montgomery, 156 Maple Road, Beaverland, IL 60515.

Elvina Allen
421 Wonder Lane
Blossom, MI 48106

Ms. Margo Montgomery
Maple Road
Beaverland

Elvina Allen
421 Wonder Lane
Blossom, MI 48106

Ms. Margo Montgomery
156 Maple Road
Beaverland, IL 60515

Activity 6

Addressing envelopes

Bring several blank envelopes to class. Address envelopes using the following information.

1. Stanley Smith lives at 2375 Cherry Lane, Squire, West Virginia 24884. He is writing to Patricia Lee who lives in Lamont, Oklahoma 70215, at 417 West Street.

2. Michael Dudley, 3245 Euclid Avenue, Detroit, Michigan 48206, is writing to Michael Harper, 201 Northland Drive, Yonkers, New York 10101.

Activity 7

Using state abbreviations

Below is a list of the fifty states in the United States. Opposite the name of each state is its traditional abbreviation. Give the new two-letter abbreviation for each state. Be sure to capitalize each letter of the new abbreviation. And remember not to use periods. The District of Columbia is also included. It brings the total count to 51.

_____ Alabama (Ala.)	_____ Oklahoma (Okla.)	_____ Maine (Me.)
_____ Arizona (Ariz.)	_____ Pennsylvania (Pa.)	_____ Massachussetts (Mass.)
_____ California (Calif.)	_____ South Carolina (S.C.)	_____ Minnesota (Minn.)
_____ Connecticut (Conn.)	_____ Tennessee (Tenn.)	_____ Missouri (Mo.)
_____ District of Columbia (D.C.)	_____ Utah (Ut.)	_____ Nebraska (Nebr.)
_____ Georgia (Ga.)	_____ Virginia (Va.)	_____ South Dakota (S.Dak.)
_____ Idaho (Ida.)	_____ West Virginia (W.Va.)	_____ Vermont (Vt.)
_____ Indiana (Ind.)	_____ Wyoming (Wyo.)	_____ New Hampshire (N.H.)
_____ Kansas (Kans.)	_____ Alaska (Ala.)	_____ New Mexico (N.Mex.)
_____ Louisiana (La.)	_____ Arkansas (Ark.)	_____ New York (N.Y.)
_____ Maryland (Md.)	_____ Colorado (Colo.)	_____ North Dakota (N.Dak.)
_____ Michigan (Mich.)	_____ Delaware (Del.)	_____ Ohio (Oh.)
_____ Mississippi (Miss.)	_____ Florida (Fla.)	_____ Oregon (Oreg.)
_____ Montana (Mont.)	_____ Hawaii (Hw.)	_____ Rhode Island (R.I.)
_____ Nevada (Nev.)	_____ Illinois (Ill.)	_____ Texas (Tex.)
_____ New Jersey (N.J.)	_____ Iowa (Ia.)	_____ Washington (Wash.)
_____ North Carolina (N.C.)	_____ Kentucky (Ky.)	_____ Wisconsin (Wis.)

Writing personal memos

Everyone uses the telephone. And almost everyone has had to leave a telephone message. Have you ever taken a telephone message? Did you tell the person who received the call what the other person said? Did you write a memo? The ability to communicate by phone is a skill you will need at home and on the job.

The job memo is often a printed form. Many times you can just check off the message that applies. But the personal memo requires very special writing skills. You have to sort out the details. Then you have to write a concise message. Many times there will be details in a telephone conversation that are not important. Friends and family often mix business and pleasure. For example, your friend calls you but reaches your mother. He wants you to know that college entrance exams will be Saturday at 10 o'clock. He tells your mother to tell you. The two of them also discuss last night's football game. Your mother even forecasts Saturday's weather. The personal message to you about the college entrance exams must be accurate. (You wouldn't want to go to the entrance exam on the wrong Saturday.) A personal message must also be concise. This means it should be brief—to the point. Read the personal memo below. Does it answer *who called? ... when? ... what the calling party said* (the message)? ... *how to reach the calling party* (the number)?

2:15

Anne,
    John called. Wants you to meet him at Peter's Restaurant at 4 o'clock. You can leave a message at 555-0170 if you can't make it.

Maria

Activity 8
Writing personal memos

Read the telephone conversation below. Then read the three memos written to Bob. Which of the three memos is the most effective? Is it Memo A ... Memo B ... or Memo C? Answer the questions about these memos.

Time: 8:00 P.M.

MARIE SANCHEZ: "Hello."

MIKE JONES: "Hello, Maria? This is Mike Jones. You remember, from college?"

MARIA SANCHEZ: "Mike ... Jones ... Oh yes. How are you?"

MIKE JONES: "Oh, fine. It's some weather in your fair city. I'm glad it finally stopped raining."

MARIE SANCHEZ: "Yes, so am I."

MIKE JONES: "Is Bob in? There's a business matter I'd like to discuss with him."

MARIA SANCHEZ: "You know Bob. He still works late."

MIKE JONES: "Yes, I remember he was always burning the midnight oil in college ... Well, perhaps I can talk with him tomorrow. Is there a number where I can reach him? I can call him at work tomorrow."

MARIA SANCHEZ: "You should be able to reach him at 555-1612."

MIKE JONES: "Fine. I'll ring him tomorrow morning—first thing. It was nice talking to you Maria."

MARIA SANCHEZ: "You, too. Mike."

MIKE JONES: "Oh, yes, if Bob gets home in the next hour, have him call me at my hotel. I'm staying at the Holiday Plaza, room 803. I'm calling from the lobby so I don't have the hotel's number. I'm sure it's in the phone book."

MARIA SANCHEZ: "I may not be home when Bob arrives, but I'll leave him a message."

MIKE JONES: "Thanks, Maria."

MARIA SANCHEZ: "You're welcome. Goodbye."

Memo A

Bob,
    Mike called. You can reach him at the Grand Plaza Hotel, room 803.
                 Maria

Memo B

8:05

Bob,
    Mike Jones (from college) called. Staying at the Holiday Plaza Hotel, room 803. If he doesn't hear from you by 9:00 tonight, he will call your office tomorrow morning — first thing. Wants to discuss a business matter.
                 Maria

Memo C

> Bob,
>
> Your old college friend called. You remember Mike Jones. He said that he would like to talk to you about something tonight or tomorrow. If you get in early enough call him at his hotel. He's staying at the Holiday Plaza Hotel. He's in Room 803 but he didn't have the phone number. I gave him your number at work. If you don't call him he will call you tomorrow morning first thing.
>
> Maria

	Memo A	Memo B	Memo C
1. Which memo(s) say(s) *who* called?	_____	_____	_____
2. Which memo(s) say(s) *when* the call was made?	_____	_____	_____
3. Which memo contains the clearest message?	_____	_____	_____
4. Which memo is the most concise?	_____	_____	_____
5. Which memo is the longest?	_____	_____	_____
6. Which memo(s) tell(s) how to reach Mike Jones?	_____	_____	_____
7. Which memo is the most accurate?	_____	_____	_____
8. Which memo is the most effective?	_____	_____	_____

Explain._____

_____

_____

CHECK YOUR UNDERSTANDING OF WRITING LETTERS AND MEMOS

1. Write a letter to New Catalog, Government Printing Office, Washington, D.C. 20402. Ask for a free copy of the *U.S. Government Books Catalog.* This catalog lists nearly one thousand of the most popular books and pamphlets published by the U.S. government. These books and pamphlets cover many subjects. You can learn which parks have the most scenic trails. You can find out how to get more miles per gallon of gas. There are lists of safe boating rules. You can get good material for writing term papers. Many of the booklets are free. Others can be purchased at low prices.

    Your letter should include the six parts of a business letter. The envelope should include complete destination and return addresses with ZIP Codes.

    Complete this activity by mailing your letter.

2. Write a personal memo based on the telephone conversation below. It is between Mrs. Cohn and her daughter's friend, Tracy Ward.

Time: 2:15 P.M.

MRS. COHN: "Hello."

TRACY: "Mrs. Cohn . . . Hi! It's Tracy . . . Tracy Ward. Wasn't the team great last night?"

MRS. COHN: "Yes, Tracy. They were sensational. And the Junior Varsity Cheerleaders did an outstanding job."

TRACY: "That's what I'm calling about. The J.V. Cheerleaders will have tryouts this evening for varsity. We will meet Coach Delaney and Mrs. Bolds at the main entrance to the gym at 4 o'clock!"

MRS. COHN: "Kathy will be glad to know it's today. I'm going shopping, but I'll leave her a note."

TRACY: "Mrs. Cohn, please tell Kathy to be on time. The doors to the gym will be locked at 4:15."

MRS. COHN: "I'll be sure she gets the message."

TRACY: "Thanks a lot. Wish us both luck. Bye."

Consumer complaints

The products and services we pay for are not always what they should be. Many times we have to complain. These complaints can be made a number of ways. You can write a letter. You can make a telephone call. You can even voice your complaint in person. What is the best way to handle a complaint? When do you call? When do you write? When do you handle a complaint in person? The answers to all these questions are found in this section. Here you will learn how and where to complain. You will apply many of the skills you learned earlier to real life situations. You will practice handling telephone complaints. You will write a letter of complaint. You will even evaluate how other people handle their complaints. This section begins with a consumer complaint vocabulary.

Consumer complaint vocabulary

WORDS TO KNOW

association   a group of people joined together for a special purpose

authorized   given the right or a license to do or sell something

Better Business Bureau   a group of store owners and business persons who join to improve local business practices

complaint   a statement that says you as a buyer are unhappy about a product or service

consumer   buyer, shopper, customer

Consumer Protection Agencies   government and volunteer agencies that try to protect the buyer's rights

corporation   a business formed by a group of people

damages   losses; legal term for money ordered paid by the court for your losses

dealerships   stores licensed for sales distribution of the manufacturer's product

exchange   return one item for another

Federal Trade Commission   government agency that enforces consumer laws; also called FTC

Food and Drug Administration   government agency that enforces consumer laws; also called the FDA

franchises   chain stores run by private persons but owned in part by a large corporation

fraud   deception; a dishonest act

headquarters main office

local in your area

refund the return of your money

retailer merchant, seller, store owner

Small Claims Court court where consumers can sue merchants, dealerships, etc. for small sums of money, usually less than $1,000

State Attorney General the state's chief legal officer

suit a case taken to court to gain a money settlement

U.S. Office of Consumer Affairs a government agency that handles consumer claims, investigates business practices, conducts studies on products, etc.

Study the list of consumer words and agencies above. This list gives you a consumer complaint vocabulary. Knowing the work of these agencies and the meanings of these words will help you when you want to make a complaint. Remember, you won't always be happy with products you buy or services you pay for. Many things could make you want to complain.

Activity 1

Match the consumer complaint words below with their meanings:

Defining consumer complaint words

_____ **1.** dealership

_____ **2.** franchise

_____ **3.** retailer

_____ **4.** Small Claims Court

_____ **5.** State Attorney General

_____ **6.** consumer

_____ **7.** FTC

_____ **8.** FDA

_____ **9.** corporation

_____ **10.** headquarters

A. the store owner

B. a court for handling claims of $1,000 or less

C. the chief legal officer for your state

D. the buyer

E. Federal Trade Commission

F. Food & Drug Administration

G. a chain store

H. business licensed to handle a certain product line

I. main office

J. business formed by a group of people

Activity 2

Using consumer complaint words

Complete these statements using the words below.

retailer	consumer
Food and Drug Administration	complaint
franchise	Better Business Bureau

1. Jennifer Jackson's mother called Riceland's Department Store with a _____ about her bill.

2. The Moore family has a Pizza World _____ store.

3. Charlene Cooper had to name the _____ when she took her complaint to Small Claims Court.

4. Melanie Ashton recently learned that the _____ could provide her with information on reading food labels.

5. Students in Milltown High's Cooperative Education program will visit the Milltown _____ _____ on Thursday.

6. Station WXKG in Barbersville has a _____ "Hot Line" for listeners to call in complaints.

Making complaints

Suppose you buy a pair of running shoes. Then you find that the store has sold you two left shoes. What should you do? There's only one logical thing to do. Take the shoes back to the store. *The first place a consumer should go with a complaint is back to the person who sold the product.* In most cases a merchant will exchange a product or refund your money. But sometimes you run into problems. For example, a merchant refuses to refund your money because you have used a product. You try to explain that when you used the product it did not work. The merchant does not listen. He still will not refund your money. A car repair shop charges you several hundred dollars more than their estimate. You refuse to pay. The repair shop won't let you have your car. A dry cleaner ruins a $200 jacket and refuses to cover damages. The service was so slow at a restaurant that you decide to write someone higher up to tell them about it.

Although most of the things you buy will be fine, sometimes you will have to make a complaint. Who do you write, see, or call? Listed here are at least *five* places you can take your complaint:

1. *Your state or local consumer protection agency can tell you a lot about local business practices.* They can tell you what your rights are for your complaint. You may be able to call them and get the answers to all your questions. If there is no agency in your city, you can always write your nearest agency. Check your phone book for the government agencies. Look under the name of your *state* or the nearest city your phone book serves. These listings will appear under the name of the state or city. Let's say, for example, that you wanted government listings for Los Angeles. You would look under "LOS ANGELES, City of." If the consumer agency is a *county* agency, you would look under

"LOS ANGELES, County of." A state agency would be under "CALIFORNIA, State of." Your phone book will give you the telephone number and sometimes the address of each government agency. It is better to start with a *local* agency. Local agencies know *local* consumer laws. And they may be near enough for you to explain your problem in person.

2. *The State Attorney General's Office* is another place to complain. This office will be in the capital city of your state. If your complaint affects a large number of people, this office might handle your complaint for you.

3. *The FTC and FDA have regional offices to help consumers with their problems.* The FTC is at Sixth and Pennsylvania Ave. N.W., Washington, DC 20580. The FDA is at 5600 Fishers Lane, Rockville, MD 20857. Even if you are able to solve your problem locally, writing these offices is still a good idea. You can send a copy of a letter of complaint you have written. This information can be used to help you and other consumers. These two offices also give you information on consumer rights.

4. *The Office of Consumer Affairs is located at Sixth and Pennsylvania Ave. N.W. in Washington, DC 20580.* If you get no satisfaction on the local or state level, write this office.

5. *Small Claims Courts handle consumer complaints and consumer cases involving fraud.* People who use this court wish to sue for small amounts of money. Suits in Small Claims Court are usually for $1,000 or less but at least $100. You do not have to have a lawyer to take your case to this court. You can represent yourself.

Always try to use the various agencies set up by city, state, and federal governments. These agencies should be able to solve your problem. However, there are other ways to deal with complaints. Some other places to go and people to see are listed below:

• *The Better Business Bureau.* The Better Business Bureau is a local organization of businesses. The bureau is interested in local consumer problems. It wants good relations with the local buying public. It can give you information about products before you buy. However, it doesn't handle complaints about prices. The Bureau can give specific information about a merchant. It is always interested in local businesses that may be dishonest in their advertising. The Better Business Bureau should be able to tell you how local stores handle complaints.

• *Your local newspaper or television station.* Some local newspapers and TV stations ask you to write or call in with your complaints. If your complaint affects a large number of people, a TV station or a newspaper may investigate this type of complaint for you.

- *The president of a franchise or dealership.* Sometimes a franchise or dealership will not listen to your complaint. If this happens, go right to the "top." Get the names and addresses of the people who own large chains and dealerships. These people often act faster than their local representatives.

- *Business associations.* Many businesses often join groups that look out for their general interests. These same groups want to know when one of their members is providing poor service. There is a national hotel and motel association. Its headquarters is in New York City. There is a national tenants organization in Washington, D.C. You can complain about an appliance to the Major Appliance Consumer Action Panel in Chicago, Illinois.

- *A lawyer.* If your complaint involves a large sum of money, you may have to hire a lawyer!

Activity 3

Handling your complaints

Match the names and organizations below with the type of complaint you think they might handle.

A. A hotel complaint
B. Ford automobile complaint
C. GMC automobile complaint
D. Tenant/landlord problems
E. General consumer complaints
F. Dry cleaning complaint
G. Comments about the programs on a radio or TV station
H. Automobile safety

E **1.** Office of Consumer Affairs
Sixth and Pennsylvania Ave. N.W.
Washington, DC 20580

B **2.** President
The Ford Motor Company
The American Road
Dearborn, MI 48121

C **3.** Chairman of the Board
General Motors Corporation
3044 W. Grand Blvd.
Detroit, MI 48202

H **4.** Ralph Nader
c/o Center for Auto Safety
1223 Dupont Circle Bldg.
Washington, DC 20036

G **5.** Federal Communications Commission
1919 M Street N.W.
Washington, DC 20554

F **6.** President
Neighborhood Cleaners Association
116 East 27th Street
New York, NY 10016

A **7.** American Hotel and Motel Association
888 Seventh Avenue
New York, NY 10019

D **8.** National Tenants Union
380 Main
East Orange, NJ 07108

Activity 4

Deciding where to go with a complaint

Answer the questions below. They will test your knowledge of where to take your complaint.

1. Who is the first person you should complain to about a product?_____
_____

2. Where do you go if you do not have a *local* consumer protection agency in your area?_____
_____

3. Where is your state attorney general's office located?_____

4. Where is the U.S. Office of Consumer Affairs located?_____

5. If you want to explain your side of a problem in court without a lawyer, what court do you use?
_____

6. If your claim is about a local store that's been running misleading ads, where should you go?
_____

Activity 5

What action would you take?

In each of the situations below list the action you would take. Would you call the store? Hire a lawyer? Contact the Better Business Bureau? Write the action you feel is best in the space provided. You may feel you should take more than one action. Be prepared to explain why you would take the action you took.

IF . . .

. . . WHAT SHOULD YOU DO?

1. Your new air conditioner needs repairs. It is covered by a warranty. The authorized dealer wants you to pay for the repairs.

_____

_____

_____

_____

2. A store keeps advertising a "Going Out of Business" sale, but never goes out of business.

_____

_____

_____

3. A furniture delivery included two damaged chairs. The delivery men said they were not responsible.

_____

_____

_____

4. The dry cleaners lost the buttons on your new coat. The owner said, "They must have been loose." He refuses to cover the cost.

_____

_____

_____

Calling with a complaint

You may decide to call a business with a complaint. Many complaints can be handled successfully over the telephone. If the newspaper delivery person failed to deliver your newspaper, a simple call should solve the problem. The drugstore delivered the wrong prescription. A call is the most effective way to correct the mistake.

When you decide to call about a problem with a product or service:

- Have at hand all the information you need to explain your problem.
- Be ready to:
  a. give your name, address, and phone number
  b. describe the events that led up to the problem
  c. give any information that will help solve the problem: a date, the name and model number of a product, the name of the person you placed an order with, etc.

Many times, a phone call is the best way to solve a complaint. But your telephone communications skills must be effective.

Activity 6

Handling a complaint by phone

Read the telephone conversation below. Then answer the questions about how the customer presented this complaint:

KATHY (counter person): Lino's Pizza. Kathy speaking. May I help you?

JOE HUME (customer): Yeah, you can help me all right. Listen, what kind of pizza joint are you people running?

KATHY: What's the problem, sir?

JOE: I ordered a pizza over an hour ago. Some guy *just* delivered it, and the blasted thing is cold. WHAT KINDA' PLACE ARE YOU PEOPLE RUNNING?

KATHY (getting annoyed): I'm sorry that your pizza was cold, sir. But don't take it out on me. We had a lot of orders to fill tonight. We're doing the best we can. Did you try sticking the pizza in the oven?

JOE: No, I didn't try sticking the pizza in the oven. I ordered a hot pizza, and I wanted a HOT PIZZA!

KATHY: I'm sorry your pizza was cold, sir.

JOE: Well, don't let it happen again.

KATHY: I can't promise that sir. Would you like to order another pizza, sir? Our Deluxe is $9.50. Our medium pizza is . . .

1. How would you rate this telephone complaint? Was Joe Hume's telephone call effective? Why or why not? _____

_____

2. What did Joe accomplish? _____

_____

3. How would you have handled this situation if you were Joe Hume? _____

_____

_____

Read the second version of the same telephone complaint. Then answer the questions about how the customer handled this complaint.

KATHY (counter person): Lino's Pizza. Kathy speaking. May I help you?

JOE HUME (customer): Yes, Kathy. This is Joe Hume at 1331 Linwood Drive. I ordered a Deluxe Pizza from Lino's over an hour ago. The pizza was *just* delivered. And it's cold.

KATHY: I'm sorry the pizza was cold, sir. But there's really nothing I can do. We had a lot of orders tonight, and we're really running behind.

JOE: Is the manager in?

KATHY: Yes, he is.

JOE: May I speak with him, please?

DAVID RYAN (manager): Dave Ryan. May I help you?

JOE: Yes, Mr. Ryan. I placed an order over an hour ago for one of your "10-minute" Pizza deliveries. I just paid $9.50 for a Deluxe Pizza that's too cold to eat. This is the second time in two weeks that this has happened.

MANAGER: What's your address, sir?

JOE: 1331 Linwood Drive.

MANAGER: Linwood Drive is definitely *within* our 10-minute delivery zone. I'll have someone drop another Deluxe Pizza order by right away. How's that, sir?

JOE: That will be fine.

MANAGER: I'm sorry your order was delayed. We've been training a lot of new people, and we're running behind in our deliveries. Things should be back to normal soon, sir.

JOE: I understand. Thank you very much.

1. How would you rate this telephone complaint? Was Joe Hume's telephone call effective? Explain why or why not. _____

_____

2. What did Joe do differently? _____

_____

3. Would you have handled this complaint the same way Joe did? If not, how would you have handled

it?_____

_____

Handling complaints in writing

Some complaints are *only* effective in writing. If, for example, there is an error on your bill, you should follow up your phone call with a letter. This letter will give you a record of when and where you wrote. It will also show what you said. It will increase your chances for ACTION. You can always give a company until the next billing period to correct an error. After that, it's time to write a letter stating the problem. You can still call, but writing will protect your legal rights.

Sometimes you need to list the events that led to your complaint. This type of complaint is also handled best in writing. When you choose to complain to the owner or president of a large corporation, write. This person is most likely very busy. The job of following up on your complaint may be given to another person. In a letter you can state your complaint clearly. You can also send copies of any sales receipts or letters. This letter can be looked at again and again until the complaint is resolved.

Activity 7
Writing a letter of complaint

Pretend you are G. W. Anderson. Write Roland's Dinnerware Unlimited. You ordered a set of china. The sugar bowl was chipped when your shipment arrived. You would like a replacement. Your account number is 8611-003-32-4. You can make up addresses. Write the Consumer Sales Department. Use today's date.

or

Pretend you are D. R. Harvey. Write Grey's Department Store. The soles on the leather running shoes you bought came apart during the first week you wore them. You want a refund, but the clerk at the store refused. The manager of the shoe department was not available to talk with you. Now you write to the store manager with your complaint. Make up a date for the purchase of the shoes. You paid $35 for them. Make up addresses. Use today's date.

CHECK YOUR UNDERSTANDING OF COMPLAINTS

Choose the best meaning for the underlined word in each of the following sentences.

_____ **1.** A dealership is
   a. a buyer
   b. a salesman
   c. a store

_____ **2.** Small Claims Courts handle cases involving
   a. less than $100
   b. $1,000 or less
   c. more than $1,000

_____ **3.** A retailer is
   a. a buyer
   b. a store owner
   c. a credit customer

_____ **4.** The Better Business Bureau is
   a. a local organization
   b. a state organization
   c. a federal organization

_____ **5.** When a person suffers damages, he or she
   a. has been injured
   b. has lost money
   c. has been arrested

Write a letter of complaint to a TV network. Complain about a program you recently saw or a change in the schedule of your favorite show.

ANSWER KEY

BASIC WRITING

Activity 1, p. 4
1. Topic: the day I disobeyed my father   Attitude: regret
2. Topic: my bedroom   Attitude: messiest room in our house
3. Topic: everyone attending last night's game   Attitude: physically and emotionally drained
4. Topic: real friendship   Attitude: value

Activities 2 and 3, pages 4, 6
Answers will vary.

Activity 4, p. 6
1. Sugar is bad for your health.
2. The effect of sugar on health.
3. Yes. (The writer tries to show through examples how sugar can be bad for a person's health. The writer only discusses the effects of *sugar* in a diet.)
4. yes
5. . . . too much sugar in your diet can affect your health.

Activity 5, p. 8
1. c (This sentence summarizes why Mrs. Marlow is respected and repeats the theme or the topic sentence.)
2. c (This sentence begins with a transition word to point out that it is a concluding statement.)
3. c (This sentence concludes the topic by taking a position based on the topic sentence. If this is true, then . . .)

Activities 6 and 7, pages 8, 9
Answers will vary.

Activity 8, p. 10
A jet engine works with only three basic parts: an air intake, a combustion chamber, and an exhaust outlet. First, air comes in through the air intake. Second, air and fuel mixed in the combustion chamber catch fire. The air and fuel mixture actually explodes in the chamber. Third, the hot exploding gases push out at great speed through the exhaust outlet. As the gases push outward and backward, the plane moves forward.

Activities 9 and 10, pages 11, 14
Answers will vary.

Activity 11, p. 17
Run-Ons
1. Roy found the missing part; it was still in the box. *Or:* Roy found the missing part. It was still in the box.
2. Sally told us the score; we could not believe it. *Or:* Sally told us the score, and we could not believe it.
3. Mrs Hill came in the classroom frowning. She had graded our midterm tests.
4. Ellen exercised for over two hours. She wanted to lose weight in a hurry.
5. I ran to answer the phone. My brother sat waiting, and my sister kept reading her book. Everybody in the room wanted me to answer the telephone.

Fragments
1-5 Answers will vary.

Activity 12, p. 20
1. Are   2. is   3. is   4. were   5. Were   6. plays
7. likes   8. wants   9. tries   10. looks

Activity 13, p. 21
1. She took a cab downtown and got out at my apartment.
2. I told him that the store was closing, but he came in anyway.
3. The teacher presented the basic format, and then she had the students fill in the details.
4. He gave an excellent performance as Othello; he really seemed to have gotten into the part.
5. The instructor came into the room, gave us a lecture, and then passed out our test papers.

Activity 14, p. 21
1. goes   2. related   3. changed   4. wished   5. likes
6. climbed   7. discussed   8. amuses   9. asked   10. used

Activity 15, p. 23
1. Jane, please come home with us.
2. Do you like playing soccer?
3. Watch out!
4. I bought hamburgers, potato chips, and cokes.
5. Joe likes football, but he dislikes baseball.
6. Although sports programs for girls are new in some schools, the teams have done well.
7. Because it was raining, the game was cancelled.
8. No, I don't like jogging.
9. Tina likes her new job, but the hours are too long.
10. M*A*S*H was on TV for eleven years, and the reruns will be on for a few more years.

Activity 16, p. 25
1. I really enjoyed the book *Anatomy of a Murder*.
2. My Aunt Ruth took me to a French restaurant with my cousins.
3. Is Austin a large city?
4. I always enjoy our family picnic at Greenland National Park.
5. The song "Remember My Name" is a top seller.

Activity 17, p. 28
1. counsel   2. principal   3. dessert   4. passed   5. lose
6. to   7. Who's   8. stationary   9. capital   10. It's
11. accept   12. altogether   13. all right   14. They're
15. there   16. piece   17. led   18. already   19. too
20. you're

Activity 18, p. 29
1. lives   2. was   3. Doesn't   4. has   5. are   6. is
7. looks   8. gave   9. is   10. are   11. carried   12. were
13. has   14. do   15. is   16. likes   17. don't
18. stopped   19. sells   20. is

Activity 19, p. 30
1. No, we shouldn't complain.
2. When all of the children are ready, we can start the game.
3. We searched for pennies, nickels, and dimes in the sand.
4. The damage to the building, however, was less than we thought.
5. It snowed all day, and the airport was closed.
6. Joe likes bike riding, swimming, and baseball in the summer.
7. I am not happy with my job, but I don't want to quit.
8. The meeting was held on Wednesday, March 9, 1970.
9. Although they practiced hard, the team was not ready for the game.
10. I am good at math, and I also like science.

Activity 20, p. 31
1. I have always wanted to visit New York City.
2. The Amazon River is very long.
3. My parakeet likes seeds and lettuce.
4. Do you like Chinese food?
5. The Afro-American Construction Company has the contract for the new building.
6. I enjoyed the book called *A Wind in the Door*.
7. My favorite TV program is As the World Turns.
8. How many German restaurants can you name?
9. I like to listen to my Aunt Liz and my cousins talking.
10. They lived on Elmwood Avenue last year.

Check Your Understanding, p. 33
Paragraphs will vary.

First News Story
spelling: received, sophomores, definitely; *punctuation:* Lake Shore High School; *wrong word:* their lives

Second News Story
capitalization: quarter; *tense shift:* returned the ball; *subject-verb agreement:* raced, took; *fragment:* The 150th . . .

WRITING LETTERS AND PERSONAL MEMOS

Activities 1, 2, 3, and 4, pages 36, 38
Answers will vary.

Activity 5, p. 41
The second envelope is correct. It includes the state and ZIP Code in the destination address.

Activity 6, p. 42

Stanley Smith
2375 Cherry Lane
Squire, WV 24884

Miss Patricia Lee
417 West Street
Lamont, Oklahoma 74643

Michael Dudley
3245 Euclid Avenue
Detroit, Michigan 48206

Mr. Michael Harper
201 Northland Drive
Yonkers, New York 10704

(Students may elect to use state abbreviations on envelopes.)

Activity 7, p. 42

AL	Alabama (Ala.)	AR	Arkansas (Ark.)
AZ	Arizona (Ariz.)	CO	Colorado (Colo.)
CA	California (Calif.)	DE	Delaware (Del.)
CT	Connecticut (Conn.)	FL	Florida (Fla.)
DC	District of Columbia (D.C.)	HI	Hawaii (Hw.)
GA	Georgia (Ga.)	IL	Illinois (Ill.)
ID	Idaho (Ida.)	IA	Iowa (Ia.)
IN	Indiana (Ind.)	KY	Kentucky (Ky.)
KS	Kansas (Kan.)	ME	Maine (Me.)
LA	Louisiana (La.)	MA	Massachusetts (Mass.)
MD	Maryland (Md.)	MN	Minnesota (Minn.)
MI	Michigan (Mich.)	MO	Missouri (Mo.)
MS	Mississippi (Miss.)	NE	Nebraska (Neb.)
MT	Montana (Mont.)	SD	South Dakota (S.D.)
NV	Nevada (Nev.)	VT	Vermont (Vt.)
NJ	New Jersey (N.J.)	NH	New Hampshire (N.H.)
NC	North Carolina (N.C.)	NM	New Mexico (N.M.)
OK	Oklahoma (Okla.)	NY	New York (N.Y.)
PA	Pennsylvania (Pa.)	ND	North Dakota (N.D.)
SC	South Carolina (S.C.)	OH	Ohio (Oh.)
TN	Tennessee (Tenn.)	OR	Oregon (Oreg.)
UT	Utah (Ut.)	RI	Rhode Island (R.I.)
VA	Virginia (Va.)	TX	Texas (Tex.)
WV	West Virginia (W.Va.)	WA	Washington (Wash.)
WY	Wyoming (Wy.)	WI	Wisconsin (Wisc.)
AK	Alaska (Alas.)		

Activity 8, p. 44, 45, 46
1. A, B, C   2. B   3. C   4. B   5. C
6. B, C   7. B   8. B   Memo B gives all the necessary information without wasting words.

Check Your Understanding, p. 47
Letters will vary. Memo must answer *who, what, when,* and *where.*

CONSUMER COMPLAINTS

Activity 1, p. 49
1. H   2. G   3. A   4. B   5. C   6. D   7. E   8. F
9. J   10. I

Activity 2, p. 50
1. complaint   2. franchise   3. retailer   4. Food and Drug Administration   5. Better Business Bureau   6. consumer

Activity 3, p. 52
1. E   2. B   3. C   4. H   5. G   6. F   7. A   8. D

Activity 4, p. 53
1. the merchant who sold you the product   2. your state consumer protection agency or State Attorney General's Office, or the Office of Consumer Affairs   3. in the capital city of the state   4. Washington, DC   5. Small Claims Court
6. The Better Business Bureau

Activities 5, 6, and 7, pages 53, 54, 57
Answers will vary.

Check Your Understanding, p. 57
1. c   2. b   3. b   4. a   5. b
Letters will vary.